The Addiction Process

The Addiction Process

A Systemic Cultural Condition

"Dr. Bob" Colonna, Ph.D., C.A.S

Writers Club Press
San Jose New York Lincoln Shanghai

The Addiction Process
A Systemic Cultural Condition

All Rights Reserved © 2000 by Dr. Bob productions

No part of this book may be reproduced or transmitted in any form or by any means, graphic, electronic, or mechanical, including photocopying, recording, taping, or by any information storage retrieval system, without the permission in writing from the publisher.

Writers Club Press
an imprint of iUniverse.com, Inc.

For information address:
iUniverse.com, Inc.
5220 S 16th, Ste. 200
Lincoln, NE 68512
www.iuniverse.com

First Printing

The Twelve Steps are reprinted and adapted with permission from Alcoholics Anonymous World Services, Inc. Permission to reprint and adopt the Twelve Steps does not mean that AA has reviewed or approved the contents of this publication, nor that AA agrees with the views expressed herein. AA is a program of recovery from alcoholism. The fact that we use Twelve Steps patterned after AA to address other problems, does not imply otherwise.

Published by: "Dr. Bob" Productions

Cover by: "Anonymous Artist"

Edited by: Sandra Little

ISBN: 0-595-14838-7

Printed in the United States of America

To all the alcoholic addicts who have passed on, and in loving memory of my brother Jerome, who was addicted and died from this disease.

Acknowledgments

I would like to acknowledge all recovering participants that were in my lectures, where the idea for this book was conceived. I am grateful for the existence of the Twelve-Step programs and the privilege of having the opportunity to benefit from their spiritual principles.

I would like to give thanks to all the people who supported me through the months of writing this book. Special thanks go to Clarie Kuball, who stood by me through difficult times; Carmen Landeros, for her patience and diligence in typing several versions of the rough draft of the manuscript; Sandra Little, for her creative editing and re-writing; and, of course, Sheila Fimreite, my significant other, who has been faithfully at my side for over ten years. Last, but not least, I acknowledge all the people that are suffering because of their past conditioning and beliefs, and I thank my ex-wife and children and grandchildren and apologize to them for not always being accessible and available over the years to support their emotional needs.

Be kind and loving to yourselves.

Contents

Acknowledgments vii
Contents ix
Introduction xi
Chapter 1   Disease and Addiction 1
   Concepts of Disease and Addiction 3
   Core Beliefs and Addiction 6
   The Progression of Addiction 11
   Categorizing Addiction 13
Chapter 2   Disease Model 15
   Biological Component 20
   Genetic and Biological Roots of Addictions 21
   Further Thoughts on the Biological Aspects
   of Addiction 26
   Psychological Component 28
   Spiritual Component 30
         The Social Component 35
   Summary of the Disease Model 36
Chapter 3   Culturalization 39
Chapter 4   The Journey Back Home 51
   The Twelve Steps Program 54
   Spiritual Dimension and Higher Power 56
Conclusion 63
Appendices 67
   Appendix I: Profile of Addiction 67
   Appendix II: Three-Step Exercise Ritual 69
   Appendix III: The Twelve Steps of AA 71
   Appendix IV: The Twelve Steps of DA 72

Appendix V: Twelve Step Support Groups 74
Appendix VI: SUGGESTED READING 76
About the Author 77
Book Order Information 79

Introduction

This book is the result of a series of lectures given by the author to participants in a chemical dependency treatment program. The topic was the addiction process and how alcohol, drug, and other forms of addiction are symptoms of a systemic cultural condition that permeates thinking throughout our society.

The intent of this book is not to do a treatise on the politics of addiction. But we cannot avoid the impact that politics and public policy have on the way we deal with the endemic problem of alcohol and other drug abuse and addiction. Current public policy toward addiction is to enact stringent criminal laws that emphasize punishment and incarceration of the user. This policy avoids the real problem and enables society's denial. The issue that we have to examine as a society is our Judeo/Christian ethic, that fundamental belief system that generates fear, guilt, and shame. Along with our cultural belief system, we are also conditioned to live under a value system that advocates principles based on our social, political, and economic systems. These two systems together give birth to the addiction process.

The addiction process is the result of an underlying generic disease that is driven by a core belief system based on a foundation of fear, guilt, and shame. This system is the product of a culturalization process that is instilled in us by the three primary institutions of family, religion, and education. The core belief system determines our reality in life and who we are in relation to life.

The genesis of the generic dis-ease and the addiction process is the separation from our *innermost self,* or soul. In place of our innermost self is the conditioned false-self that is the product of beliefs and old ideas of the culture we were born in. In the addiction process the false-self learns to avoid the feelings of pain and powerlessness caused by our core beliefs by creating a false sense of reality. This distorted reality gives the illusion of security in an insecure world. The illusion of security becomes an *avoidance pattern* and *comfort zone* to protect us from our core beliefs of *fear, guilt,* and *shame* that are part of an addictive thought system that reinforces the addiction process.

When we compromise the insecurity of our true self in favor of the security offered by the false-self, we have a new belief system that is driven by the addictive thought system that believes it is possible to control everything in life, including people, places, and situations, other countries, and even outer space. It is a thought system that believes we can play God—to know, understand, and control everything. It is a self-centered thought system that tells us we are a separate superior species, with a self-endowed covenant to control all creatures and natural resources of the world to meet our needs and expectations.

A by-product of this addictive thought system is alcohol, drugs, and other addictions. Society's lack of awareness of the underlying generic disease sees drug abuse and addiction as a morality issue that is eating away at the very fabric of our culture and our way of life. The reaction by society and government is the so-called "War on Drugs," attacking primarily illicit drug use and possession with aggressive legislation that incarcerates criminals and users for months or years in jails and prisons. The rationale for these aggressive laws is to make our community "safe" by getting "these people" off our streets. Recent statistics indicated that one out of three African-American males are caught up in a criminal justice system on some level, either jail, prison, probation, or some other. Over 60% of the cases are alcohol and drug-related crimes.

We have now lost three generations of our young people to nicotine, alcohol, and other drugs, and to a criminal justice system that incarcerates and stigmatizes them as criminals—a label that can follow them for the rest of their lives. Unfortunately, our laws make a definite distinction between alcohol abuse and drug abuse. Our culture has a long history with alcohol that is very similar to that of nicotine. It has become a socially accepted drug, even though it has contributed to more deaths than any other drug, save nicotine. Society and our legislatures, overtly or covertly, defend the use and advertisement of alcohol. This is reflected in the disparity of our criminal laws, which mandate lesser criminal penalties for alcohol offenses and more extreme penalties for other drug use and possession offenses.

A recent study released by the National Center of Addiction and Substance Abuse of Columbia University stated that alcohol is more closely associated with crimes of violence than any other drug. Twenty-one percent of state prison inmates incarcerated for violent crimes were under the influence of alcohol and no other substance when they committed the crimes. Violent crimes among jail inmates are also more closely linked to alcohol than to any other drug, with 26% of convicted violent offenders under the influence of alcohol alone at the time of their crime vs. 4% under the influence of crack or cocaine alone, and none under the influence of heroin.

These eye-opening statistics make one wonder whether the social acceptability of alcohol and the inequitable criminal penalties for alcohol abuse and drug abuse have any underlying racial tones. The drug alcohol, like many of today's illicit drugs, was introduced by the white man and has a long history as primarily a white man's drug; the other drugs, such as cocaine, crack, and heroin are popular with people of color. This theory is substantiated in the 1996 statistics describing racial and ethnic disparity in our prison population. Half of all inmates in state prison for drug offenses are African-American and 26% are Hispanic. In the state and federal prisons African-American inmates are most likely to have used crack in the month before their arrest, and Hispanics are more apt to have used heroin or cocaine.

At the end of 1996, more than 1.7 million American adults were behind bars, over 80% of them for alcohol and drug-related crimes. This statistic does not include juvenile offenders who are in our juvenile halls. The majority of people in prison are persons of color, are poor, and have committed drug-related offenses. The war on drugs has no significant long-term effect on the reduction of drug use and sales and has not been a deterrent to new generations of youth who are now taking over where the previous generations have left off.

Until we as a society understand and accept that alcohol and other drug abuse and addiction, like many other forms of addiction, are the result of an underlying generic dis-ease that is systemic within our culture—with physical, spiritual, and social ramifications—and cannot be solved by criminalizing the disease, this viral endemic condition will continue to spiral to the point of losing our humanity.

Society's fear and government reaction to that fear is a result of the lack of understanding of this endemic disease, which has polarized and disenfranchised a whole segment of the population with its harsh criminal penalties and social stigmatization. We as a society have closed our minds to accepting addiction as a disease, just as we have with other physical and mental diseases in our history, where the victims have been morally judged and banished. We would like to see addicts disappear. Our prisons have become islands that keep the "upstanding citizens" separated from the prison population, not unlike the leper colonies of the past. This is the only disease that we punish someone for having.

Our prisons and jails are bursting at the bars with alcohol and drug abusers and addicts and those who sell illegal drugs. The lack of quality treatment in our prisons and jails if any at all, will only continue the revolving door syndrome filling our prisons and jails with repeat offenders. A large percentage of crimes that are committed in America are directly or indirectly alcohol and other drug related. It is time to stop fooling ourselves on what is politically expedient and accept the fact that if we as a nation is going to have a chance to mitigate the increasing crime rate we have to make a larger investment in our public health system and provide treatment programs on demand. In addition to treatment we need to offer supportive housing programs, job training and education and social living skills as a holistic approach to treatment and recovery.

Recent studies have shown that treatment on a multiple needs approach is less expensive and more successful than incarceration. We need to reconsider whether punishment is a more effective long-term approach to the alcohol and other drug problems than a multiple need approach to treatment and recovery.

Our federal government and local governments, in addition to law enforcement agencies and the general public, need to realize that alcoholism and other drug addiction is symptomatic of a larger problem, which comes from a sickness that is rooted in the thought system of our culture. Finding the solution will begin with treatment in our healthcare system and *not* the criminal justice system. The ultimate solution will come with a major paradigm shift in our societal thinking that actually will become a spiritual awakening.

In this book we will explore the bigger picture of alcohol, drugs, and other manifestations of addiction and see how they are aspects of an addiction process that is a systemic condition within our culture, and how the root of the problem goes to the core of our cultural thought system that forms the beliefs, ideas, and attitudes of our society and its institutions. We will explore the disease concept of addiction and how it is multidimensional, with biological, psychological, spiritual, and social ramifications. If we are going to sincerely confront this problem, it will be necessary to approach it on all levels, beginning with the understanding that addiction is not a criminal justice problem, but a public health issue, and needs to be addressed by a cooperative effort of community support organizations; i.e., churches, self-help groups, counseling, etc.

Until there is an honest and sincere public debate on the decriminalization of drugs, the criminal justice system needs to serve as a deterrent and play a

collateral role in encouraging and reinforcing treatment and recovery within the health system.

We also cannot ignore our family of origin and the influence it has on childhood psychological development. Most of our dependencies and addictions stem from wanting to control inner feelings by manipulating people, things, and events in our life. Much of the need to do this arises from childhood, from the experiences we had in our families—the lack of acceptance, and our most basic need for love and nurturing that were inadequate in our early childhood years. Our parents and caretakers in many cases were not emotionally available for meeting our needs; this had an effect on our emotional and spiritual development and the individuation process toward self-hood, which later in life becomes the root of our adult dependencies and addictions.

In the following pages we will examine our primary cultural institutions; we will see how religion has contributed to our core beliefs of fear, guilt, and shame and has had an impact on our psychological development. We will also examine our educational system and its lack of creative nurturing. It is time to reevaluate these primary institutions and see how they have influenced a value and thought system that has created a foundation for spiritual anorexia in our culture, resulting in a society that is at dis-ease and which is seeking to feel at-ease through attachments, dependencies, and addictions.

Finally, we will examine the largest self-help recovery program in the world—how hundreds of thousands of people have changed their lives by practicing 12 spiritual principles in their daily lives, (the Twelve Steps). These spiritual principles become a wake-up call to show us how powerless we are over what happens in life, our past, in our dependencies and addictions, and how by practicing these 12 spiritual principles we can begin to understand that surrendering to our powerlessness will bring empowerment and change in our attitude toward life.

We are in the midst of a crisis that is tearing away at the very essence of our humanity. A drastic change is needed—a paradigm shift in our status quo thinking that so desperately clings to old values and beliefs by resisting substantial change that can free us as human beings to the natural forces of conscious evolution.

The time is now for a cultural revolution—a renaissance, if you will, as we enter a new millennium. Let's not wait until we lose a fourth generation of youth to alcohol and other drug addictions and to a criminal justice system of juvenile halls, jails, prisons, or death. It is time now for all of us as individuals in a society to make a commitment to recovery, which means recovering from our past, to a new way of thinking that will encompass the trinity of our humanness, our *being – self – human*, or spirit-soul-body, that will become our path to self-realization. This book is a step in that direction.

Chapter 1

Disease and Addiction

Concepts of Disease and Addiction

I first became interested in addiction about 16 years ago. At the time I was working on my personal recovery and studying for my Ph.D in psychology counseling. My original interest was in alcoholism because I had a long family history of alcoholism and was contemplating doing research and counseling in alcoholism. I was deciding on a research topic for my dissertation and was curious about why the word disease was used in reference to alcoholism.

I was aware that the American Medical Association proclaimed in 1957 that alcoholism "was a medical condition and considered a disease." The proclamation was accompanied by a detailed medical definition that was directed to medical professionals and not the general public. So I decided to pursue my own research and started with the word "disease." I began by going to the Webster Dictionary to look up the definition for disease. Mr. Webster said, *"Disease is anything which interferes with the human organism's ability to function in a normal way."* I have always been uncomfortable with the word "normal." I don't understand what it actually means. If I am normal, then everyone has to measure up to me to also be considered normal. And who is to say that I am normal? The same could be said by using the majority behavior of society as a baseline measure of normal. Who is to say that the majority of society's behavior is normal? Anyway, I replaced the word "normal" with "in a healthy way." So now the definition reads,

*"Disease is anything which **interferes with** the **human organism's ability to function in a healthy way**."*

Now that I understood the definition of disease, I took the next step, which was to find the definition of "addiction." Webster had an incomplete definition, defining addiction as a "habit," which to me is not really accurate. The Webster Dictionary and psychiatric and medical dictionaries gave definitions of addiction that were limited in scope, didn't satisfy my idea of a definition that would be understood by a lay person, and also didn't encompass all the forms of addiction. So I decided I'd have to do a little more work and research the various studies in journals to see if there were definitions of addiction used in these studies. There were several studies over the years and several definitions. Some were lengthy, some were technical, and others were not as complete as I would have liked. I decided to take portions of various definitions that I thought were useful for my research, added some to my own definitions, and finally came up with a composite definition of addiction that I felt would describe the term in a broader sense than the common definitions. This is the definition I came up with: *"Addiction disorder is a chronic, progressive condition characterized by the loss of control to obsessive thinking that manifests into compulsive behavior toward any mood-altering substance and/or activity."* I felt this definition encompassed all the forms of addiction, ingested and non-ingested, and what has been noted in the addiction field as "process addiction" vs. "substance addiction."

It was then time to examine whether my definition of addiction was commensurate with the definition of disease. Let's examine the definition of disease again and see if there are correlations with the definition of addiction. *"Disease is anything which interferes with the human organism's ability to function in a healthy way."* If we examine the definition of addiction and underline those key words that correlate with the underlined words in the disease definition, we can decide if addiction could be considered a disease: *"Addiction disorder is a chronic, progressive condition characterized by the **loss of control to obsessive thinking** that **manifests into** *compulsive behavior to any mood-altering substance and/or activity."* The underlined portion of the definition of addiction correlates with the key words in the definition of disease, which are the determining factors.

First we have the "loss of control to obsessive thinking." This phase would be consistent with the definition of "interferes with the human organism's ability to function in a healthy way." From this we could conclude that the "manifestations of compulsive behavior" could also be an obstacle to "living in a healthy way." Both of these definitions of addiction could be considered commensurate with the key portions of the disease definition. And we could conclude that addiction does fit the definition of disease and can therefore be considered a disease like diabetes, heart disease, and any other disease. What's important to understand is that the key portion of the addiction definition comes down to the *powerlessness in our thinking,* which results in *powerlessness in our life.* In my opinion, this powerlessness in our own thinking is responsible for the wrong choices and decisions that make an addict's life unmanageable and is inherent in the disease of addiction.

Since the AMA's proclamation in 1957, several research studies were done on cocaine, heroin, and other drugs, and also on non-ingested compulsive behaviors that were found to be addictions. As we continue to pursue this subject you will begin to understand how ingested and non-ingested compulsive behavior is commensurate to the definition of addiction.

Core Beliefs and Addiction

In our society we tend to see addiction as a dependency on alcohol and other drugs that manifest a behavior that is irresponsible and destructive. Most of us do not understand that what we call chemical dependency and other addictions grows out of a *generic cultural dis-ease* that is inherent in the system in which we live. It is a *dis-ease process* that is built on a foundation of attachments and dependencies that is integrated in our daily routine as coping mechanisms for living life. I call this the *addiction process*.

The generic cultural *dis-ease* originated from the separation from our *innermost self*, or *soul*. It is reinforced and maintained by a core belief system that permeates thinking throughout our society. Just by being born in this culture we are all affected by the generic culture dis-ease and a part of the addiction process. The difficulty that many of us have in accepting our addiction is the fear of looking inside ourselves for what we might discover. What we will discover is our attachment to core beliefs and old ideas that are unconscious forces that drive the addiction process we live in.

Addiction is more than being dependent on mood altering substances and behavior. It is much deeper than our biological or environmental influences. The root of addiction grows from the primary components of the generic cultural dis-ease: *fear, guilt,* and *shame*, which are conditioned childhood fixations that become the underlying force that controls our thinking process. The conditional fixations become our core belief systems. A belief is something we were taught to hold true. It is what we use to interpret or misinterpret the world around us. So, if our beliefs are inaccurate, they become restrictions that limit our potential in life. Our beliefs can actually deter us from reaching our highest potential and greatest good, if they are inaccurate interpretations of the way life really works.

Holding inaccurate beliefs is like being inside a room with no windows. We can only see four plain walls and a closed door, like a prison cell. Unfortunately, the instructions on how to live a full and meaningful life are on the outside of the room. We would have to develop the courage to walk over to the closed door and open it. It sounds like a very simple thing to do, but when you are not aware that opening the door is a possibility, it is not an option. It is not within our limited conscious reality to see the door as a way to perceive life differently because of the attachment we have developed to our core beliefs that have become our coping mechanisms for living life. As we cling to attachments they become our comfort zones and avoidance mechanisms from our emotions and feelings. The attachment and comfort zone adaptations can become manifestations of various forms of addiction.

Most of us experience some form of addiction by the very nature of being born in this culture. Many of our social institutions contribute and force feed into the addiction process by way of bombarding our minds with judgments, criticisms, seduction, and expectations on how we should look, feel, and think. This is done through various social institutions and the media. It all began in our family of origin as children, and in our schools, through peer pressures, and in religious values. This influence continues into adulthood, in marriages, in relationships, in the workplace, with family members, and last but not least, in the media, which glamorizes many addictions with advertisements that promote the expectations of the perfect image, creating desires and unnecessary needs, encouraging overconsumption, and magnifying fear. It is part of the addiction process that feeds into our core beliefs of fear, guilt, and shame that undermines any attempts for change or recovery.

As a way of avoiding the feeling of inadequacy and lack of fulfillment caused by our conditioned belief system and also our societal pressures or expectations, we seek out pleasures by fulfilling our desires and needs with compulsive object attachments to people, places, situations, and things, including alcohol and other drugs. In many cases this behavior can develop into manifestations of many forms of addictions.

Addictions are desperate attempts to develop comfort zones through our compulsive attachments as a way of avoiding pain, unwanted thoughts, feelings, emotions, fears, and anything we prefer to avoid.

Some of the feelings, emotions, and fears that we would like to avoid and replace with comfort zones of pleasure are:

loneliness and powerlessness
escape from the past and future
feeling the void or emptiness

Many of the avoidance mechanisms that we develop with comfort zones begin with a pattern or routine surrounding an activity, situation, or substance, which become, in many cases, an unconscious or conscious fixation on something outside ourselves as a way to avoid our inner feelings and thoughts. The routine can then become object attachment that can progress to compulsive behavior and addiction.

The pattern includes four steps:

1- routine   2-attachment   3-compulsion   4- addiction

Just think of the many routines that you are attached to in your life. Make a list of them on paper and apply the four steps to each routine to see what level of progression it is on. You may be surprised how unconscious you are of one or more routines and how, knowingly or unknowingly, you have progressed to a level of attachment, compulsion, or addiction. The one that comes to mind for me is my morning coffee and newspaper ritual, which I indulged in for many years. This simple innocent routine led to attachment over the years and finally developed into a compulsion and addiction.

Most of the progression was unconscious to me; I had no awareness of my dependence on this daily morning activity. I found out it was an addiction when my work schedule changed and I did not have the time to participate in this activity any longer. When I made the change in my daily schedule I immediately felt the physical reaction to the withdrawal from the caffeine and the emotional withdrawal from not reading the morning paper. This with drawal continued until I adapted to a new morning schedule.

Any attachment that we have difficulty letting go of because of the withdrawal effects and the void or emptiness that is left in its place can be considered a dependence or addiction to that activity, situation, place, or substance. Because of the nature of addiction, it is considered a progressive condition or *dis-ease* from levels of mild to acute, and eventually, to chronic. We give our addictions priority over other things in our lives, where it becomes a ritual that we pay homage to, like serving a god. We live in the illusion that the addiction is serving a purpose in our lives until eventually it stops working and we transfer to another addiction or get help. Addiction to our beliefs is at the core of all addiction. Most of us substitute one addiction for another.

Take a few minutes and examine the list of your routines. Choose one of your more prominent routines that you may feel is an attachment. Now, imagine letting go or detaching from that attachment, whatever it may be, and visualize living your life each day where you have detached or totally eliminated the attachment and see how that makes you feel. If you have difficulty imagining living without the attachment or having detrimental physical and/or emotional feelings around letting go of the attachment, it may be because you have some degree of addiction.

The fear of the consequences to any detachment can be from the expectation of the void or vacuum that is felt in its absence and the fear of loneliness because of the loss of a relationship to the attachment. It is similar to my morning ritual of reading the newspaper and drinking several cups of caffeinated coffee. When I detached from that daily activity, I not only experienced the physical withdrawal symptoms from abstinence, but also the loss of a relationship I had with the morning ritual. The point I am attempting to make is the attachment to anything that has mood-altering effects become our comfort zones and coping mechanisms of avoidance from feelings, thoughts, and emotions that are driven by our conditioned core beliefs of fear, guilt, and shame.

Our past conditioning leads to our beliefs, and they have a controlling effect on every aspect of our lives. We are what we believe. The beliefs we have about ourselves and our lives affect the choices and decisions we make in our lives. They have ramifications on all levels, from how healthy or unhealthy we are, to how successful or unsuccessful we feel about ourselves. We can empower beliefs to heal or kill us.

Empowering inaccurate or false beliefs to control our lives can lead to illness and addiction. One common behavior produced by our false beliefs that is directly connected to our childhood relationship in our family of origin is to be a *people pleaser,* as a way to get people to like and accept us. This comes directly from the deep feelings of being unaccepted and/or unloved children. And because we feel unaccepted and unloved, we try to control people, situations, and events in our life that make us feel good about ourselves. That gives us the illusion of power.

Unfortunately many of the choices and decisions we make because of the influence of our core beliefs usually have detrimental long-term effects and are due to some level of addiction. In many cases this is an unconscious addiction process that is characteristic of our conditioned false-self, which is a product of culturalization, an enslaved victimization process.

We can create several comfort zones of avoidance by our attachments to people, places, situations, substances, and activities. These object attachments are encouraged and reinforced by the societal and institutional values that feed into the addiction process. This part of the addiction process is what I call the *addictive thought-system,* and almost all of us on some level are affected and controlled by this thought system, which is based on our conditioning and learning. The detachment from the addictive thought-system is a difficult thing to accomplish because the social, economic, religious, and political forces in our society are resistant and unsupportive of detachment. In fact, they encourage and support attachments and dependencies. The campaign of fear and insecurity is the nourishment that fuels the addictive thought-system, which is a restraint to our freedom. It keeps us shackled to the bondage of addiction.

Because of the complexities of the generic cultural dis-ease, I will give you an overview of the progressive levels of manifestation. The genesis of the dis-ease starts at the *moment of birth*, when the separation begins and is followed by the *culturalization*, a conditioning and learning process that becomes the foundation to the development of *false-self*. We are influenced by the fixation of core cultural beliefs and old ideas that are indoctrinated in our minds by our primary social institutions of family, religion, and education, to become products or commodities that will be obedient to the socio-political-economic value system of society. The primary core beliefs become our shackles of bondage through our obedience to *fear, guilt,* and *shame.* These core beliefs are reinforced through our years of childhood psychological development, and later they contribute to the unconscious neurosis of our society.

The generic dis-ease is a cultural systemic condition that progresses to the level of individuals' addictions.

The Progression of Addiction

1 *Generic dis-ease*	< >	*Separation*
2 *Addiction Process*	< >	*Core Beliefs*
3 *Addictive Thought-System*	< >	*Distorted Thinking*
4 *Individual Addiction*	< >	*Bondage Self*

Our past conditioning has caused us as a human species to separate from our essence or innermost self, our spiritual calling, if you will, to a level of the loss of our humanity. Our past conditioning led to our beliefs, that give us our dis-ease with life and give birth to an addiction process that relentlessly seeks a feeling of "ease" through various forms of addiction.

Categorizing Addiction

I think many counselors in the addiction field, as well as the general public, are guilty of what I call categorizing addiction. I feel that the self-help 12-step programs, for all the good that they bring to an addict's life, also contribute to *categorizing*. We categorize addictions according to a person's drug of choice or activity, such as alcoholic, cocaine addict, heroin addict, food addict, sex addict, and so on. I realize that the purpose of individual labeling is to confront the addict with the primary addiction and its connection to the problem of living. But unfortunately, when we do this, we are also giving that person a double message that's saying, once you're abstinent from your primary addiction, you have overcome your problem.

We addicts will stretch an inch into a yard if the opportunity arises. I was working with a so-called cocaine addict who said cocaine was his problem and he was able to drink beer and smoke marijuana on occasion without a problem. My response to him was, *"Maybe you can drink beer and smoke grass once in a while and it won't be a living problem"* (even though I had reservations about saying this) *but eventually you will begin to abuse alcohol and marijuana, or the alcohol will bring you back to your drug of choice. This will happen because you are a chemically-dependent person who is afflicted with the disease of addiction."* Intellectually he understood what I said, but he was not emotionally ready to accept it. This incident is a good example of what we call in recovery *"stinking thinking,"* which means that the addict is in denial of his disease.

In defense of Alcoholics Anonymous, I need to add that when it started in 1934, it was organized around the concept of alcoholism. At the time, other drugs were not a major societal problem, especially in the white community where AA began. It made sense during these early years for members to introduce themselves as alcoholics. But now times have changed and other drugs, in addition to alcohol, have become a major societal problem. Poly-addiction is more the norm today than the exception. This issue will become clearer in the next chapter, the Disease Model.

Chapter 2

Disease Model

Addiction is a multi-dimensional disease that affects us on every level of our being. This is what makes the disease so complicated and so difficult for us to understand. An effective treatment program needs to address each dimension or component of the disease (see Fig. 1).

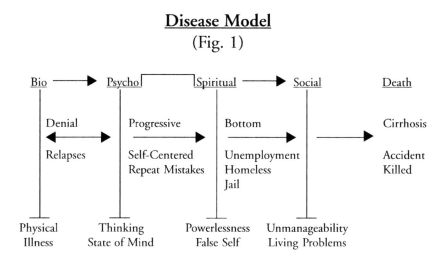

Disease Model
(Fig. 1)

Many different methods have been used to treat addiction. Before the 1960s, addiction was treated as a mental health disorder, and alcoholics were placed into state hospitals and mental institutions. Bill W., the co-founder of Alcoholics Anonymous, had several long stays at mental institutions and was put in straitjackets. Alcoholics were placed in straitjackets during the withdrawal process because doctors thought they were experiencing some kind of psychotic episode. They didn't realize patients were experiencing alcohol-induced seizures.

In 1957 the American Medical Association proclaimed that alcoholism was a medical condition and a disease, and in the early 60s, they gradually stopped putting alcoholics in mental institutions, but they still didn't know what to do with them. Many were sent to acute care hospitals or sanitariums and were treated as though they had a medical condition. But many of us realize now that it's more than just a medical condition. Through research, we're discovering that this disease affects every part of us. It has a *biological* component to it, which is the physical illness. It has a *psychological* or mental component that determines the way we think and our state of mind. It also has a *spiritual* component, which I will elaborate on more fully as I explain the disease model. Finally, it has a *social* component: the culmination of the disease has social ramifications—the self-destruction in our life, the unmanageability, the unemployment, the loss of family, the loss of relationships, and even jail. These are the results of hitting bottom.

If only one component of the disease is dealt with, you're solving only part of the problem. Because many professionals have not used a multifaceted approach to the healing process we, in my opinion, haven't had much success in treating the disease over the years, and there's been a high rate of relapse. After months, and sometimes years, of abstinence and sobriety, one relapses. I've known people who have had five years and ten years of abstinence and sobriety, who relapse. Why?

Many find this difficult to understand. The disease is complex, and for many years the medical profession didn't want anything to do with it. They threw it back to the lay community. That's how, in 1957, 12-step programs started prospering. They, and some religious groups, were the only ones who would deal with this complex disease. Some psychologists and psychiatrists experimented with traditional psychotherapy, medication, and psychoanalysis using "talk therapy" and behavior modification techniques, but all of these approaches had little success in comparison to AA, with its self-help meetings at which alcoholics supported one another's sobriety using the spiritual principles of the 12 steps. The co-founders of AA, Bill W. and Dr. Bob, who were chronic drunks for many years, found that talking to each other on a daily basis supported them in their endeavor not to drink. They decided if it worked for them, it might work for others, and that's how it all started.

Alcoholics Anonymous and other 12-step programs became global self-help organizations that saved hundreds of thousands of lives. The development of the spiritual principles of the 12 steps became the core of the programs' healing process.

Biological Component

The first component, the biological component, has been accepted in the field of addiction for many years. To this day there are some treatment professionals and even self-help programs that view the biological component as the primary component of the disease, the effects of which cause psychological symptoms. So, why is addiction considered a physical and biological disease?

Genetic and Biological Roots of Addictions

I would like to refer to the chart that I call "The Inborn Biochemical Defect/Genetic Propensity" (fig. 2). If we look at the chart and follow Pathway 1, for a person who does not have the genetic propensity to alcoholism, we can see that when the alcohol is ingested it is metabolized into acetaldehyde, which is a by-product of alcohol and is highly toxic.

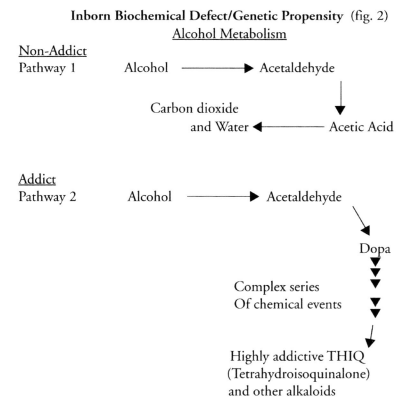

The results of this toxicity are usually experienced the morning after a night of alcohol abuse, with symptoms of headache, nausea, and physical weakness. Acetaldehyde is in the same chemical family as formaldehyde, which is used for embalming corpses. The liver is the organ that detoxifies toxic substances, and when the liver is overloaded, it begins to malfunction, and some of the toxic residue stays in the blood system that circulates through our body. If alcohol and other drug abuse continue for several years, cirrhosis or hepatitis B and C can result from overload on the liver.

The acetaldehyde is broken down into acetic acid (vinegar) and then it is broken down into carbon dioxide, which we breathe out, and water, which we eliminate through urination. The alcohol is completely eliminated from our system within 24 to 48 hours because alcohol is a water soluble drug.

Now let's look at Pathway 2, which shows what happens when someone who has the biochemical defect drinks alcohol. The acetaldehyde interacts with *Dopa (Dopamine)*, a brain chemical that is a neurotransmitter. Dopamine is one of the brain's "feel good" chemicals, which help us with mental clarity and movement to cope and function in our daily living. The brain produces a certain level of dopamine for us to function in a healthy way. The dopamine and acetaldehyde then go through a series of chemical events, which transform into a chemical that is called *Tetrahydroisoquinalones* or THIQs. These have high levels of addictive properties, similar to morphine and heroin, but much more potent.

THIQs were discovered about 10 years ago. A research study was completed on brain tissue biopsies of John Doe alcoholic and heroin addict corpses in public morgues. The research found levels of THIQs accumulated in the brain tissue that do not metabolize. A fat-soluble chemical can stay in your system for several weeks to several months, much like marijuana. In Pathway 2, lcohol is converted from water soluble to fat soluble.

The results of the human brain tissue biopsy study motivated further studies with THIQs' addictive qualities in animal behavior. The study included rats that were exposed to an alcohol solution of vodka, sugar, and water, on one hand, and plain water on the other. The rats preferred the alcohol solutions and continually drank them to the point of intoxication. This protocol was used for a period of several weeks until the rats were conditioned to alcoholism and would only drink the alcohol solution and lose interest in food and water. A brain biopsy indicated high levels of THIQs.

In a subsequent study, a different strain of rats was used and was exposed to the same alcohol solution, and plain water as an alternative. These rats would not drink the alcohol solution and instead drank the water. They seemed to be resistant to alcohol and could not be conditioned to alcoholism. So the researchers injected THIQs directly into the brains of these rats. They synthesized THIQ in the laboratory and injected it into the rats' brains. They put the rats in the cage again and led them to the alcohol solution. The rats started drinking the alcohol solution and didn't stop until they all dropped dead. They wouldn't stop drinking. They wouldn't eat, or drink water. They just kept drinking the alcohol solution until they overdosed, in this case, to death.

This study showed the addictive strength of the THIQ. Obviously the doses these rats were given were probably 50 times the dose that a human would have, but it is an indication of why an alcoholic does not stop after one drink. You don't stop until you're totally intoxicated, blacked out, or some intervention takes place—sometimes death. So it is the THIQs that cause that physical craving of wanting more and more and not feeling satisfied because as you drink more, the THIQ levels go up and you want still more. That's the nature of addiction.

This is merely some of the research that has been done primarily with alcohol and heroin. These studies provided proof of a definite biological component to alcoholism and heroin addiction that may be connected to an inborn biochemical defect or genetic component. Since these studies on alcohol dependency have been concluded, research has been done on other mood-altering drugs such as cocaine, marijuana, and heroin, which also indicated a genetic connection similar to that found in the case of alcoholism.

Scientists at a recent conference announced the results of a study that had identified some of the genes associated with drug abuse. The study described the mutations in those genes that led people to abuse certain types of drugs, such as marijuana, heroin, cocaine, and others. This landmark discovery brings us closer to understanding the physical component of the disease of addiction. Currently, the scientific community agrees that genetics are involved in drug abuse. It is thought that multiple genes act together to make a person more likely to abuse drugs. Since the disease of chemical addiction appears to be the product of both heredity and environment, the roles of the two are inseparable and interact with each other.

Whether someone feels good after smoking marijuana is strongly influenced by heredity. The above study's conclusions were based on 352 pairs of identical male twins and 255 pairs of fraternal male twins—all of whom had smoked marijuana more than five times in their life. Identical twins have identical genes, fraternal twins have approximately half the amount of identical genes. The researchers concluded that genetic factors have a significant impact on whether someone will enjoy marijuana.

Another discovery relates to neurotransmitters of the brain and the presence of seratonin deficiency in alcoholic addicts that were at low levels when they were in abstinence, and as soon as they used, the seratonin levels went up. Seratonin is a mood regulator neurotransmitter that helps us to sleep at night. Nature has provided enough seratonin in our system to keep us balanced. But when we have seratonin deficiency, we are out of balance. Seratonin deficiency and dopamine are found to contribute to depression; this is another reason why we find a lot of dual diagnosis in recovery. We'll find someone with a chemical addiction problem and also depression. People may ask, "What comes first, the chicken or the egg?" Was the depression there early in that person's life, leading to medicating with alcohol and drugs to relieve the depression, or is it the other way around? It's hard to say, but we know there is a connection; depression goes along with the disease.

Prozac and other psychotropic drugs are seratonin and dopamine uptake drugs. They basically increase the levels of these two substances. When you increase seratonin and dopamine levels you mitigate depression for some people. Alcohol and drugs do the same thing. They increase the seratonin and dopamine levels, so when people use, they can overcome their depression. When a person is abstinent, they go into depression and have to go on medications, sometimes psychotropic drugs, to balance themselves so they're able to stay in recovery and not relapse. There is a high relapse rate with depression after abstinence. That's a big factor. The body can take several months, even two or three years after abstinence for seratonin levels to return to normal. During that time, you could be relapsing if you're not on medication. Therefore, sometimes medication is needed for some people temporarily, to help support their sobriety.

The results of this study substantiate the old recovery slogan of AA: "once an alcoholic/addict, always an addict." There is no cure from the disease of addiction, but there is progress in overcoming the control the disease has over our lives. As a recovering alcoholic of 25 years, if I were to drink today, I wouldn't start all over again as a beginning drinker and progress over the years into a chronic drinker. I would fall right back to the level of drinking I was at when I went into recovery; that's why we say in recovery that the disease is always there, the biochemical imbalance is always there, it is only in remission.

Further Thoughts on the Biological Aspects of Addiction

Now we have a better understanding of the physical aspects of the disease, why it is a physical disease, and why we need abstinence to neutralize it. Again, the disease is not the substance. The disease is not even the THIQs. They are merely the symptoms of the disease. What we have to do is neutralize the biological component of the disease, meaning that abstinence starves the disease. What alcohol and drugs do is nourish the disease—keep it alive and well, by keeping the THIQ level up and the seratonin level up. So long as everything is up, you're feeling fine. But as soon as you stop using, everything goes down. It's this roller coaster life. Up and down, up and down. We get caught up in that cycle of addiction.

So the object is to neutralize the biological component of the disease by abstinence. I envision the disease as an entity within us that sort of goes to sleep. When I'm in abstinence the disease is like a bear that goes into the cave in the winter and hibernates. It goes to sleep. As long as I don't feed it anything, it will stay asleep. But as soon as I begin to give it any kind of stimulants it is going to wake up. When I say stimulant, that means even substances like caffeine and nicotine, which can keep the disease partially awake. When I say caffeine I don't mean one cup of caffeinated coffee a day, but five, six, seven, eight or more cups a day. That becomes a very strong stimulant that your body has to detoxify. You get withdrawal symptoms when you stop; you get headaches when you're withdrawing from caffeine, so that tells you that it is an addictive drug because our bodies have to withdraw from the stimulation effects.

Nicotine is another subtle drug that will keep the disease alive and vulnerable to relapse. Most people in recovery get to the abstinence point and then they go no farther. Because in most cases they think that is the problem, and as long as they don't use, they're fine. But you're *not* fine. It's more complicated than that. You've only dealt with part of the problem. You may be abstinent and attend 12-step meetings and still relapse periodically.

In our abstinence we may intellectually admit we have a problem with mood-altering substances and other addictions and understand that we should abstain from their use and/or participation. But, like many of us addicts in early recovery who are not really convinced that we can never use or participate in any addictions, we think that someday we *will* be able to use our addiction again in a controlled way. This kind of thinking suggests that willpower is the antidote to the obsessive/compulsive symptoms of addiction. Every time I talk about this or hear someone who has a history of chemical dependency and addictions talk about willpower as the answer to long-term sobriety, I remember a statement made by someone who is a motivational speaker and an "old timer and an alcoholic." He said, ". . .*alcoholism has as much to do with willpower as diarrhea.*" Did you ever try willpower to stop yourself from going to the bathroom when you had diarrhea cramps? I'm sure if you are insane enough to try, you will find that it doesn't work.

We need to understand that when we get into thinking that our willpower can control our addiction, we are in denial of our disease. It is a total lack of understanding of the disease because if we really understood it, denial would not exist. You face the reality of it whether you like it or not. You realize that it makes no sense in denying what is, and if you don't accept this disease that you are afflicted with, you will continually experience relapses, and your problems of living will not change.

Why is abstinence not the resolution to our problem of chemical dependency and other addictions? The answer is that there is more to the disease, and abstinence is only half of the problem. There is the psychological component, which is directly related to the spiritual (see Disease Fig. 1 chart), but for clarification, I will talk about the psychological component separately.

Psychological Component

There is a definite connection between the psychological and the spiritual dimensions of ourselves. That is why I speak of the psycho-spiritual component of the disease. The psycho-spiritual dimension of the disease model interacts with the biological aspect of our thinking and becomes an obsession and the driving force behind the choices and decisions we make in our lives. It leads us down the path of self-destruction. It affects whom we choose to marry or partner with, and whether we're going to have children. It affects the kind of career or employment we choose; in fact, it affects most of what happens in our lives. It's our state of mind that is the foundation that controls our thinking and becomes our bondage or enslavement. This is where our powerlessness over our addictions comes from. This is the dis-ease.

Mood altering substances or activities also play a role in the psycho-spiritual dimension of the disease. This may be surprising for some of you to hear, especially after we've been hearing for so many years that addiction to mood altering substances is a physical condition or a physical disease, and once you abstain from the substance(s), your problem is resolved. Sorry to disappoint you, but that's not entirely accurate. As I continue to explain the multi-dimensional model, hopefully you'll begin to have a better understanding of the cause and effect dynamics of the disease of addiction.

A concept that helped me understand the differentiation and interconnection of the biological and psycho-spiritual component is that there is a biological defect in the way we metabolize alcohol and drugs. It's the part of the disease that causes the physical craving for the substance. However, the biological component is in the latent state until we make a choice to take the first drink or use the drug. This is when the psychological component comes into play. The manifestation of the disease doesn't begin with the biological component, which the medical profession, and some alcohol and drug counselors, have believed for many years. This has been gradually changing over the years, but there are still many recovering individuals who hold the belief that alcoholism is only a biological disease.

I'd like to make clear that I do not refute the fact that there is a biological component to the disease, but as I said previously, it is only part of the problem. In my opinion, and the opinion of a growing number of others in the field of addiction, there are other dynamics of the disease that primarily contribute to the activation of the biological component or biochemical defect, and one of these components is psychological. The biological component is secondary. It's the medical condition the AMA refers to in its 1957 proclamation, which defined alcohol as a disease. The psycho/spiritual component is also the disease, so I guess you can say the addiction is a disease of dis-ease.

The initial symptoms of chemical dependency or any other addiction is found in one's thinking and state of mind. Our powerlessness in our lives begins with the way we think, and this in turn determines the choices and decisions we make in our lives. The results of our thinking is the foundation of our living problems, which become the "*bondage self.*" Then we have to ask the question, "Where does this thinking and state of mind come from?" The answer is that we've been conditioned to be addicts the moment we left the safety of the womb. This may surprise some of you who may have thought the problem of addiction was just a bad habit or a way of coping with the difficulties of life, or just a way of having a good time and overdoing it once in a while, or, last but not least, just making us feel better. These are just a few excuses one makes in an attempt to rationalize addiction. These excuses are not totally inaccurate; they're symptoms of our problems, not the cause of them. We are the product of our culture, which formulates the value system and foundation of the society we live in. I will talk about this more fully in the next chapter.

Spiritual Component

What I will share with you in this section is my opinion and theory that stems from studying the words and experiences of many individuals of higher consciousness who have walked the path to self-realization. It is not something you have to accept or believe unless you feel that it makes sense to you. The only thing I request is that you keep an open mind and are willing to process the information to determine if there is anything you want to keep.

The Triune of Humankind

Life begins to unfold at the moment of conception, when the sperm unites with the egg in the process of physical creation, when *Spirit*, or a *God Force*, incarnates in humankind to become the first part in the trinity of becoming human. The *Spirit* represents our *Being* and contains the configuration of the *Soul*, or *Self*, that is yet to be born. At the core of the Soul/Self is the *Sacred Seed*, which contains the potential blueprint of our individuality, purpose, and destiny that we bring to the world.

This purpose can be as simple as what I am doing right now. I share and extend myself and bring information to people like you that may help you turn your life around. You never know. It could just be one word or one statement that I make that can effect a shift in your life and in your thinking. Your purpose may be to create a child who may become a scientist who will discover the cure for all cancers in the 21st century. Who knows? Or it may simply be someone you touch by saying a word as a friend that makes a big difference and changes a life. It can be just the little things that we never pay attention to. It's not just the holy people from the various religions who effect change. It takes everyday people like us, who contribute to life and enrich it by our own individual uniqueness encapsulated in our Sacred Seed.

The process starts with our *Being*, that slowly evolves and unfolds from birth and continues through our psychological, physical, and spiritual development into adulthood. During this process the *Being* gives birth to the *Soul/Self*, which becomes our individuality in a process that is divinely created to continually evolve toward *Self Realization*. The third entity of the trinity is the *Human* aspect, which represents our physical existence in the world. Our uniqueness as human beings is the pre-existence of the *Self*, which continually unfolds and integrates with the human aspect of ourselves as we experience life. The *Self* is developed as a result of *Becoming Human*. It is the core entity of the trinity of *Being-Self-Human*. It is a process of evolving consciousness and awareness toward *individuality* and *self-awareness*.

When we come into the world the *Being* aspect of the trinity is the manifestation of spirit or God that is incarnated in the unconscious. We are born as unconscious "Beings" with no sense of outward consciousness or objective consciousness, other than the subjective instinctual senses of hunger, thirst, pain, sleep, and safety. The infant is functioning primarily from the lower reptilian part of the brain, similar to animal instincts.

In some esoteric and religious circles, the unconscious part of the psyche is considered the realm of spirit or God, who gives birth to all creation. The deity aspect of the psyche, our potential "Self", is born from the womb of the unconscious. It is encapsulated in the Sacred Seed that is in the incubation state waiting to unfold and blossom. Within the Sacred Seed is what I call our spiritual DNA, which is not unlike the physical DNA that determines our gender, body form, and intellectual potential. There is biblical reference to the Sacred Seed in the Gospel. The Gospel of Matthew in the New Testament speaks of the kingdom of God as a mustard seed planted in the soil of consciousness. The kingdom of God is in us as a seed that we bring into the world at birth, planted in the ground of our "Being," which is God or spirit from which everything grows.

The false self, or personality, which is the product of our cultural conditioning, blocks our ability to accept or understand our sacredness. The personality is like a prison that keeps our innermost self in bondage. Most of us as children experience true freedom of our essential self from birth until the age of seven or eight. The separation from our innermost self begins as the personality takes hold of our behavior. In a few short years the personality becomes stronger and gradually we begin to lose that childlike innocence, the spontaneity and freedom that comes from the connection to our innermost self. It becomes a time where we completely forget that part of us and forget how to return home. This is the cause of much suffering in our lives. We will be able to understand when we surrender to a power greater than ourselves and trust that this "Higher Power" will show us the way. The ability to understand is the key that can unlock the door to the prison of suffering and help us to a new life. In each of us is a seed of understanding; that seed is God. If we doubt the existence of that seed of understanding, we doubt God.

I sense that the "Being" part of our three-fold entity is in the image of God, or saying it another way, godliness is part of our three-fold identity. It is the part of us that is described in Genesis, when God created the world and made humankind in his image. I would like to think that when the "God Force" created the world, it made all creation in the God image. I have always felt that the term human being was really backwards and should be, "being human." We are already "beings" when we come into the world. Our journey of life in this world is all about learning how to be human. In the process of learning how to be human the resonance between the interplay of "being" and "human" is the birth of the evolving, unfolding of the "Self", the center of our trinity. The primary purpose of living in this world is to move toward completing the trinity of ourselves. The process of integration with our three-fold entity is a way of becoming complete and experiencing God or Spirit as one with ourselves. This is sometimes called Self-realization.

The various descriptions of the human triune are shown in Fig. 3, **The Human Being Triune**.

Being—Self—Human

God—Soul—Body   = Self Realization

Nature—Seed—Matter

Unfortunately we do not live in an ideal world, where the forces of cultural and societal thinking are supportive of or consistent with the integration of the triune process toward self-realization. Somewhere in the process of the evolution of consciousness, we have lost our way and separated from our spiritual source of who we are and replaced it with a conditioned or false self that sees the physical world as a place to satisfy our desires and wants. There is a biblical story called "The Fall of Man," that is a good example of the results of this kind of thinking. This is the story of Adam and Eve in the Garden of Eden, where greed and self-centeredness resulted in the banishment of Adam and Eve to a world of duality, where good and evil and suffering and pain exists.

The human species developed an ego/personality to replace our true nature and divinity, which has taken control of our lives. It is similar to the temptation and control the serpent had over Adam and Eve. Being under the possession of the false-self is the cause of our separation from our God-self; it is what causes the bondage of pain and suffering. If there is any sin in the world, it is the sin of separation from our God-Source. When we lost our way we went against our own "being." Going against it is committing suicide of our innermost self, opening infinite possibilities. Life is like an empty painter's canvas; it becomes whatever we paint on it. We can paint pain and suffering, or we can paint joy and bliss. The choice is ours; we can choose the freedom of our divinity or the bondage of our ego/personality.

The disease of addiction is a spiritual problem. In the 12-step programs it is understood that the underlying problem of our addiction is spiritual bankruptcy. This becomes very clear when you understand and accept the multi-dimensional concept of addiction.

The root cause of all addictions is the separation from our spiritual source, the innermost self, or God, whatever concept you feel comfortable with. It is not important what concept you prefer; the important issue is that the separation begins at the moment of birth into a culture of established beliefs and old ideas that are promulgated and enforced through society's primary institutions of family, religion, and education. These institutions never allow the Sacred Seed to unfold and blossom. They never allow the Seed to have a fertile soil where it is watered and it can grow. Instead, they intervene and condition us to be what they want us to be, and so the Seed becomes dormant and is replaced by a conditioned false-self that becomes the identity that determines our reality. We're just actors acting out a script that was given to us, like a Hollywood movie.

So long as we have this false-self, we're going to have this feeling of powerlessness. We are powerless because we are not connected to our spiritual dimension. As long as we feel powerless, we're vulnerable to this disease of addiction. Step 1 of Alcoholics Anonymous says that we are powerless over alcohol and other drugs, but it goes beyond this; we are powerless over our past that controls our present reality. This distorted reality controls the thinking and decisions we make in our lives, and the only way to free ourselves from this mental or psychological bondage is to awaken to our spiritual dimension. Later I will talk about how this spiritual journey can begin.

The Social Component

The social component and ramifications of the disease of addiction are very obvious. If there is no intervention in the progressive nature of the disease that will get the addict into treatment, the self-destructive lifestyle will continue to a bottom line that can result in loss of employment and family, prison, illness, even death. So the social component, having to do with manageability, might be called the catch-all component of the disease, in which the chaos in our life is illuminated.

Addicts into their disease live their life like an accident waiting to happen. They never know what's happening day to day because of their obsessive compulsive behavior. Step One of the 12 Steps addresses this aspect of the disease by admitting how powerless we are over alcohol and other drugs. We are powerless over our past conditioned thinking that is the genesis of all our addictions. The social component points up the consequences of our actions from our dis-ease, of our trying to find "ease." It's what determines our "bottom line," whatever that may be, even death.

As long as we are in bondage to the false-self discussed in the last section, we will continue to feel that sense of emptiness and incompleteness that will be the driving force for seeking out satisfaction in life with substances that offer a false sense of fulfillment, such as alcohol, drugs, food, people, places, and things. And eventually, the emptiness and fulfillment disappears and the cycle begins again. It is the disease of dis-ease.

This cycle of addiction will continue until the pleasure from the mood-altering does not exceed the emotional pain that we do not want to feel. This is usually the "hitting bottom," when we become vulnerable and either reach out for help or take our chances and continue with our addiction and risk death.

Summary of the Disease Model

Referring to the disease model back in Fig. 1, the biological component for chemically dependent persons is usually the initial component of the disease or physical illness that manifests outward symptoms that are observed by others. It is the component that blows our cover and reveals the personality disorder that separates us from the general population who are not chemically dependent. It is the part of the disease that causes the intervention that gets most of us into treatment. It represents the disease of physical dependency.

The psychological component reflects the effects of the culturalization process that initiates the separation from our innermost self or true nature and replaces our identity with a conditioned false-self. This process begins at birth and continues throughout our childhood. It becomes the foundation of the *dis-ease* aspect of the physical disease that is the driving force of the addiction process, a systemic condition of our culture. The psychological component *piggy-backs* with the spiritual component that completes the dis-ease of the disease, causing unmanageability and living problems.

The spiritual component represents the loss of separation from our spiritual dimension that is our *Beingness* that we bring to the world. Within our Beingness is our spiritual essence where the soul rests, and at the center of the soul is our *Sacred Seed*, which encapsulates the blueprint of our unique individuality and spiritual purpose and destiny. But because of our cultural conditioning, which has caused damage to our psychological development in childhood, we separated from our true nature. This is what I call *Spiritual Bankruptcy*, our inability to have a relationship with our true nature, other people, and life or a Higher Power. The spiritual bankruptcy reinforces the separation and false-self identity with the feelings of low self-worth that seeks fulfillment outside ourselves with people, places, things, situations, and behaviors. It is the component that identifies the disease of dis-ease and all forms of addiction as a spiritual problem. Our spiritual void is the prison that keeps our true nature in bondage.

Chapter 3

Culturalization

Culturalization is a conditioned way of thinking and a state of mind that manifests a behavior that is amenable to a certain value system that in turn determines the lifestyle of society.

We have been culturalized and socialized in the way we think about the world and ourselves. Our reality of life is the product of beliefs and old ideas that we had nothing to do with. We were born in a culture that had existing institutions that promulgated beliefs and ideas that had fundamental influences on our life. The three institutions that had the most profound effect on how we think and our state of mind are family, religion, and education. (See fig. 4). I would like to discuss each of these institutions because it is important for you to understand how they have influenced and molded you into the person you are today, and how they contributed to the dysfunctional thinking that became part of our psychological development and a primary component of our dis-ease.

It all starts with the fact that we are born in a culture that is driven by an addictive thought system that gives us messages that money is a sign of success, more is better, survival of the fittest, divide and conquer, and us against them (see fig. 4).

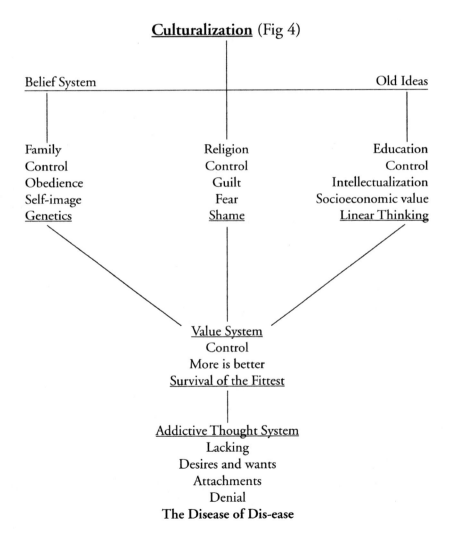

We enter the world by being born to a family who become our primary caretakers. The first people that we experience after birth are usually our parents and then other family members. At this point in our life our parents havetotal power over our psychological development. They represent the first phase of the culturalization process and lay the foundation for our defuture psychologicalvelopment. They begin to condition us to become cases their intention does not work out to be for our own good and instead can become damaging to our psychological development. This shows up later in psychological problems.

I remember when my mother would beat me for something I did that did not meet her expectations and then said, "I did this for your own good." Instead, it damaged my self-esteem to a point where I became rebellious and self destructive throughout my childhood and into adulthood. All the major decisions I made in my life were influenced by my broken self-esteem, and the sad thing is that I had no awareness of the influence my childhood conditioning had on my present life. I was no different than anyone else who just accepted that what happened in life is just the way life is, and there is nothing we can do about it. But later in life, after years of self-destructive behavior and "hitting bottom", I realized that my perception of myself and the reality of life has to do with the way we think, and if you want to change your life, you need to begin by changing the way you think.

Before this process can begin you have to first understand how your childhood psychological development was influenced extensively by our family system and other institutions of our culture. They conditioned and sculpted us like computer software that commands the computer to respond to the operator's wishes. In our childhood we had no power over who we were and what our identity would be. We were at the mercy of our family system, where we experience *powerlessness* for the first time in our lives. I have always thought that the resistance many recovering people have to accepting Step 1 of the 12 Steps of Alcoholics Anonymous is a reaction to our childhood feelings of powerlessness.

The greatest tragedy of life is breaking the spirit of our children. We destroy their naturalness and replace it with a false-self that conditions them to conform to one way of thinking. The culturalization and indoctrination of the core beliefs of *fear, guilt,* and *shame* rob our children of their innocence. There is a *breaking of spirit*, in which children are controlled by fear and through obedience, and where they lose their naturalness. Wildness is synonymous with naturalness. I also feel that wildness is synonymous with freedom. The wild horse is identified with "free spirit," which is exemplified when the horse is in its natural habitat and roams and runs freely on the hills and plains. We intervene in this natural habitat and capture wild horses with a rope around their necks. The horses are then corralled, and the conditioning process of "taming" begins. The word used is "broken." The wildness or naturalness is broken, to a level of obedience. In this conditioned state, the horse responds to the command of the master. This is not unlike what was done to us as children and continues to be done.

Once the foundation of our cultural conditioning is in place through the family, we become exposed to the other two institutions of influence on our culturalization, which are religion and education. In many cases, at the age of five or seven we are exposed to religion and the indoctrination of a God who is watching us at all times, with certain rules and expectations for us to abide by. If we refuse or fail to live up to these rules and expectations, this God will become disappointed and even angry. We are looked upon as sinners who need to repent our sins if we want to get back into the "good graces" of God. This kind of religious propaganda reminds me of the Santa Claus myth, in which we were told that Santa watches over us all year to see if we're good or bad children. If we didn't meet Santa's expectations of what is good, we would get a lump of coal in our Christmas stocking instead of presents.

Religion and myths such as the Santa Claus myth are closely related; both are ways of controlling children, teaching them to march to the beat of the drummer. That drummer happens to be the values of Judeo/Christian culture, which is endorsed by our families and reflect the value of society. These values are so much a part of the collective psyche of our culture that which specific religion you practice is irrelevant.

The next institution we are exposed to is the education system, which, next to the family, probably has the greatest influence on our thinking. Our educational system is designed to teach us the principles and values of the socioeconomic system under which we live, which is a capitalistic driven economy that is based on a philosophy of "survival of the fittest." This is similar to the theory of evolution, where the strongest survive and the weak die. The difference is that the theory of evolution refers to the natural change or cycle of birth and death and not an artificially manipulated economy, where the cards are stacked in favor of the few who have the power to influence our socioeconomic values through the political process. The present traditional educational system indoctrinates us to the values of our socioeconomic system, which prepares us to be a supply source for the business corporate culture, conditioning us to fit into a corporate world. If you get a job, you fit in.

I envision that our culture is like a big puzzle, and all pieces of the puzzle are designed to fit. There are pieces of this puzzle that are "seconds" or have defects and do not fit anywhere. You've got all these empty spaces in the puzzle and you're trying to find where they fit. Some pieces almost fit, but not exactly. The pieces that don't fit the puzzle, we discard as misfits. We throw them aside and keep looking for pieces that will fit. These misfits are alcoholics and drug addicts; they are the gays and lesbians in the community. The misfits are immigrants and slow learners, and we discard them. People that have learning disabilities are discarded because they're too expensive to take care of. The elderly are misfits that are no longer productive. We're just looking for productive people that will feed the corporate system and march to the beat of the corporate drums; i.e., profits, profits, and more profits. So if you don't fit into this puzzle, you are discarded. Addicts are misfits because society sees the disease of addiction as a stigma. Addicts are seen as losers and criminals. Society equates addiction to crime because so many addicts are in the criminal justice system. Addicts become the misfits that don't fit in, and I think this has a diminishing effect on our society. We're losing a lot of talented and creative people who can contribute to our society in many different ways.

The three primary institutions, family, religion, and education, determine what our conditioning will be and what our identity will be. As our consciousness evolves and we become self aware, we begin to know ourselves according to what we've been conditioned to think. The sad part of this is that we had nothing to do with the process of it and who we've become today. In effect, we've been conditioned and programmed by somebody else. Somebody else wrote our life script, and we're acting it out on the stage of life. We're marching to the beat of the drum, and we don't even know why.

We wonder why our life sometimes feels unfulfilled or why we feel confused, why we sometimes feel a sense of emptiness within ourselves. I've always felt that emptiness. I don't know if you have ever identified that within yourselves, but I felt that sense of emptiness for many years growing up as a teenager, feeling as though I was incomplete. I felt something was missing, and I didn't know what it was. At that age you're immature. So when I began experimenting with drinking vodka screwdrivers and I had that first drink, all of a sudden I felt alive. I felt whole, whereas before I had felt incomplete. I immediately knew this was the magic formula that was going to fix me. It progressed to the point of becoming a crutch in my life, and then it became my bondage. I became enslaved to it. It starts off as your friend, and then it turns on you and becomes your enemy. That's what addiction is.

Addicts believe that the emptiness, the lack of fulfillment that we're feeling in our life, can be filled with people, places, and things—with drugs, alcohol, food, men, women, sex, parties, new cars, houses, money, marriage, and babies. We think all these things are an immediate gratification that will make us feel better, make us happy, and that we'll discover happiness outside ourselves somewhere. And it actually works for a while, but then the emptiness returns. We repeat the same mistakes again and again, and this becomes the cycle of addictive thinking.

This is the component of the Disease Model where we are not at *ease* with ourselves, and in our search for ease, we walk down the path of self-destruction because of our distorted thinking. We are seeking out the feeling of ease through our addictions, the mood-altering effects of which give us a sense of ease, briefly, but once the ease disappears, the pain, fear, and guilt return, and the cycle begins again, until we hit our bottom. This is where we've tried everything, exhausted all remedies. We're sick and tired of being sick and tired. We've decided that everything we've tried to do to attempt to control our life didn't work. Then we reach a point of desperation, where intervention occurs in our life: getting pulled over for a DUI, getting busted for whatever reason, and now you're caught up in the criminal justice system. This is followed by an ultimatum from an employer to either get help or lose your job. Then there are ultimatums by family members or spouses. Whatever it may be, that intervention has to happen. Hopefully this is our bottom, where we now get into recovery and are ready to accept our disease.

We need to realize that we were all born into a culture that's driven by an addictive thought system that gives birth to individual addictions. We have ingested substances such as alcohol, drugs, and food that we become addicted to. Then we have what I call *process addiction*, which is work, sex, relationships, gambling, etc. These are all *non-ingested addictions.* There are many forms of addiction—the alcoholic that is the workaholic as well, the drug addict that's also a sex addict, or the alcoholic that is a relationship addict, or a gambler. We usually have our primary addiction and other secondary addictions that take many forms. Underneath all of this is a cultural thought system that makes us vulnerable to these individual addictions because of the messages in our programming from family, religious, and educational institutions. These messages tell us we're never enough, so we're always trying to be more than who we are. We're trying to measure up. We want acceptance, not only by our families, but also by our peers and employers. We want to be accepted by everybody who we feel is important to us.

We're always trying to achieve perfection. Our system tells us that the more money we make, the more successful we are. Material things are symbols of success—the kind of car we drive, how big a house we live in. We get the message that "more is better." We get messages that say only the stronger and more intelligent survive; others become casualties in our society. All these messages are addictive stimuli—addictive kinds of thinking. We have become a society of fast-track overachievers. That's very well accepted. There are certain addictions, especially process addictions, that are acceptable, even praiseworthy, in our culture. We idolize workaholics. We view them as successful. Somebody who works 60-80 hours a week is considered responsible, dependable, and a good employee. That person will go far in life. You can be successful being a workaholic and give your soul to the corporations.

So we have all this kind of thinking in our culture that is part of our programming. Now picture this scenario: if you already have the biological, genetic propensity for addiction and then you have this psychological conditioning from an addictive thought system that is rooted in our culture, you're doomed! There is no way that you cannot be afflicted with the disease of addiction. With these two ingredients, it's just a matter of time before you are going to start experimenting with drugs and alcohol and other forms of addiction. As soon as you start experimenting, after a period of time you become chemically addicted because you have the biological propensity and the foundation for the addictive thinking and the state of mind that is cultivated from an addictive thought system that is based on *lacking*—there is never enough.

The only difference between us and the rest of the population, the so-called non-addictive people, is that we possess this biological component, and most people don't. Everybody else in our society has this psychological component, but they *look* good. It's the biological component that makes us look sloppy, that gets us in jail, where the criminal justice system intervenes, or where we lose our jobs, family members, marriages, or children. It's the biological component that perpetuates the insane thinking. But the biological component is at the mercy of the psychological component that triggers it. Once triggered, the biological component becomes the power, the driving power of the disease. The psychological was the primary component, but as soon as you took that first drink or started experimenting with drugs, you gave that power to the biological component, and it takes over. It takes the "thinking" to use, but after you use, the biological component starts the craving to use more and then perpetuates on its own. It keeps the addictive thinking alive. The inborn biochemical defect will propel itself. So we can understand why these two components work together and reinforce each other, and if we don't deal with both of them, we are not dealing with the entirety of the disease.

In the last chapter I will talk about what we can do to help rid ourselves of *dis-ease* and discover the things that will help us find *ease*.

Chapter 4

The Journey Back Home

The way back home to spiritual essence is through a recovery program of lifestyle change designed to rediscover our true nature and lost selfhood, where for the first time in our lives, we become human being instead of human doing. We begin to see through the illusion of control and power that is created by the distorted thinking of the false-self that gives us the impression that we can control everything in life. The false-self gives us the message that we can live life on our terms regardless of the means that justify the ends. Once we experience a spiritual awakening we begin to realize that living life on life's terms is in harmony with our true nature; it gives us the feeling of "ease" instead of "dis-ease."

The Twelve Steps Program

The aim of 12-Step recovery is to show you that you are not alone. It enhances the "spiritual journey" by applying the steps to our daily lives and increases our ability to attain moments of oneness in relation to people, nature, and a Higher Power through meditation and prayer rather than from mood-altering substances and/or activities. In essence, the Steps are a behavioral transformation in our thinking approach to spirituality; they attack the world view or reality of the addict who has dismissed any belief in a power greater than himself as a protective object or concept for immersion and connection, other than the addictive substance and/or activities.

Recovery begins by unlearning everything we were conditioned to learn and believe and by addressing our addictions and the separation from our innermost self. It all begins with the first three steps of AA, with Steps 1 and 2 as the contemplation steps and Step 3 as the decision step that takes us toward recovery. The first three steps also stand for honesty, openness, and willingness, which are the necessary ingredients for a strong foundation of recovery. They stand for the *how* of recovery.

Step 1 represents *honesty*—identifying the problem and acknowledging the powerlessness your past thinking has instilled in you and recognizing how your lives have become unmanageable. Step 2 represents *openness*—accepting the problem of powerlessness and unmanageability and acknowledging a power greater than self-will. Step 3 represents *willingness*. This is the decision step that separates adolescence from adulthood. It is the key that will unlock the prison door and set us free if we have the courage and trust to decide to take action.

Now you are ready to work on a recovery program. Steps four through nine are action steps to prepare you for a new life. Steps ten through twelve are maintenance steps to reinforce recovery and help you fulfill the spiritual hunger that gnaws at you. They keep you centered and focused on spiritual principles in your daily lives, instead of on your former practices of misusing food, sex, money, or chemicals.

Stimulating a spiritual awakening requires a change in thinking and new learning that removes the inner blocks that inhibit growth and transformation. The Twelve Steps Program is the vehicle that can bring us back home.

Spiritual Dimension and Higher Power

When we are ready to trust and surrender to a power greater than ourselves, we will return to our true nature and begin the metamorphosis from camel to lion. The camel is trained to be subordinate to external commands to service the human master; the lion represents the freedom, courage, and strength to enter the unknown, where the innocence of the child exists. When we return to innocence, the doors of existence open up, and we find wisdom and a love affair with life.

We as a culture need to discover and respect the divinity of our "Being" by learning the self-parenting of unconditional care, acceptance, and love that is the nurturing requirement for the Sacred Seed to unfold, blossom, and grow into the self-actualized and realized three-fold human being. This is not only a requirement for infants and children, but for all of us. It is never too late to awaken and find the path that leads us home to our spiritual source. It's all about the evaluation and expansion of consciousness and learning how to be human by experiencing the center or core of our trinity, the "Self", that continually evolves when a fertile soil of self-acceptance and love is provided during the process of our human experience of living life. This process will happen if we as a culture recognize and acknowledge the fact of our separation from our divinity and are open and willing to bring a spirituality into our lives that is all encompassing. It requires an awakening to the acceptance of the wildness and naturalness of all aspects of life as the manifestation of the *sacredness of God.*

We are all born with a potential for creativity, an inner genius. This creative inner genius is in our true nature as spiritual beings. It is at the core of our "Beingness." It is part of the Sacred Seed. We come to this world from the higher dimensions, which are the same dimensions that give birth to the universe and all its creations. We are part of a divine plan and cosmic harmony that is the driving force of evolution. This means that at the time we were born, we came with everything we needed as spiritual beings to have a human experience. The sad thing is that most of us were not allowed to have this experience in the way that was in harmony with the divine plan because our culturalization conditioned us to be obedient to the social order that is structured on certain beliefs and old ideas.

The definition of obedience is: "when one gives in to the orders or instructions of one in authority or control." This implies and relies on a temperament that submits easily to control or that fails to resist domination. It suggests a weakness of character that allows one to yield meekly to another's request or demand. So by definition, obedience is a form of restriction or compromise to your naturalness or spiritual DNA, which is contrary to creativity.

This whole idea of culture and society comes from social order and wanting to civilize society. The definition of civilized in the Webster Dictionary is: "to bring or come out of a primitive or savage condition and improving in habits or manners." How arrogant can a definition be that arbitrarily evaluates another way of living as primitive or savage? It determines that another lifestyle that is different is somehow inferior and inadequate. When you look up the definition of civilization, it is defined as a social organization of a higher order, marked by the development and use of written language and by the advances in the arts and sciences, government, etc.

Can you imagine the arrogance of saying that a different lifestyle is primitive and undeveloped in language, arts, and sciences? The so-called primitive cultures are enriched with the arts, music, and dancing, as religious and spiritual rituals are at the core of their being. It comes from their freedom to be natural or true to their nature, where all creativity emerges. We are realizing more than ever today, for example, how we can no longer ignore the practice of herbal medicine and other natural healing modalities that have been successful for hundreds and thousands of years in so-called primitive cultures.

We as individuals need to unlearn everything we have learned from our culturalization of beliefs, ideas, and values. When our beliefs are based on our own direct experience of reality and not on notions offered by others, no one can take these beliefs from us. Until we stop taking refuge in our attachments and addictions in order to avoid confronting our real sorrow and inner turmoil that is the result of our past experiences and beliefs, human suffering and misery will continue to be a dominant force in our lives. We must experience the two-foot drop, from the head to the heart, where our divinity rests. It will take an unconditional and humble surrender to a God of your understanding, a total acceptance of our true nature/self and the renunciation of the false self. When we touch the reality of our true essence, we also touch the ultimate dimension of being, and become free from fear, guilt, shame, attachment, illusion, and craving.

The "Gift of Sobriety" is received when we return to the innocence of the child. Jesus said, "that unless you are reborn as a child, you cannot enter the Kingdom of God." This passage tells me that until we are ready to surrender the false self and discover our true nature of God-Self, we will continue to experience a life of suffering and pain.

The vehicle that will help us return to our childlike innocence and true nature is living our life in accordance with spiritual principles. Our cultural generic dis-ease of separation and the manifestations of addictions is a spiritual problem or emergency that needs immediate spiritual CPR. This is the beginning of the healing process that will lead us to the solution or spiritual awakening.

Learning and knowledge come from our personal experience of practicing honesty, openness, and willingness in all our daily affairs and extending ourselves to life and the world. We begin this process by developing an open and meaningful relationship in the *vertical,* i.e., person to higher power. This means that we have to feel that there is a power greater than me, greater than you. If you ever have a question about that, try what I do. In the evenings I go out at night and look up at the sky and stars, the moon, and some of the planets. Then I get in this state of awe, just watching the vastness of all this—how it is synchronized; that everything is in its place; that the sun comes up every morning, and that the night comes every time the sun sets. It is synchronized like a cosmic watch. So having a vertical connection means knowing that we are all a part of this vastness. We are all links in this universal chain. And when one link is missing, the whole universe is diminished. That's how important and unique everything is in nature, all creatures of nature. The human being, the plants, the stars, the moon, the planets, the rocks, the soil, the clouds are all links in this universal chain that keeps everything synchronized and in harmony and wholeness. So our vertical connection is being part of this wholeness, knowing that we have this interconnection and interdependency with everything in existence. It is learning how to have a relationship with a Higher Power.

To accomplish this I utilize the first three steps of AA that show me how I can build a working relationship with this Higher Power. My Higher Power is an ever changing process, rather than an object or concept. It is my conscious experience with the present moment that is always changing. It is my experience and relationship with the "Moment Reality" that continues to unfold and raises my awareness of, my connection to, and interdependence with the wholeness of life.

My relationship of oneness with my Higher Power is like that of ocean waves with the ocean. I am like the wave that rises and falls on the surface of the ocean. Some waves are higher than others, which exemplifies how we separate from our source. At times we get caught up in the world of desires and wants, and our false-self or ego perceives us as independent and separate from everything in life. Other times, we feel more connected with the spiritual aspect of ourselves. The greater the storm, the higher the waves. We are all part of the Higher Power, or God, like the waves are part of the ocean. Peace of mind and sanity comes when the storm is still.

If you go underneath the ocean there are no waves, only stillness. As we begin to change our thinking of desires and wants into a thinking of "gratefulness", our false-self/ego will diminish, and the waves will subside.

When we experience this inner peace in our lives, we begin to feel our connection with the "Infinite." We are one with the ocean of God. The ocean is always pulling the waves back from which they came, going home to the oneness of the vast ocean of Divine Love.

In addition to establishing the vertical connection with a Higher Power, we must establish the *horizontal relationship*; i.e., the person to person dimension of our lives. I touched a little bit on that when I was discussing the vertical connection, where I had this interdependency with you, my own species, the human race, where I need the vegetation, the trees.

When I think of spirituality, I think about my feelings and my relationship with myself and how I extend that relationship in life. For example, if I am watering plants in my backyard or in the house, I do it because I am obligated to water them, and I also feel good when I water them. It is obvious that the "feeling good" is a more spiritual feeling than the obligation. When we do something because we're obligated to do so, in many cases our focus is on responsibility and self-centeredness. But when we act out of a sense of identification and connection, the behavior is more holistic and natural. When I water the plants and feel good about it, I am not only nourishing the plants, but I am nourishing myself. It is similar to the principle "giving is the same as receiving." If I am giving, no matter whether it is money, a present, a service, or a favor, I am doing it out of fulfillment to myself, with no expectation of anything in return. This is what a spiritual horizontal connection means to me—a sense of interconnection with the totality of life.

The vertical and the horizontal dimensions together are what make us whole human beings because we are in both worlds. We're in the human world, the third dimensional material world, and we also are beings that are in higher dimensional worlds, the spirit world. So we can say that the three facets of human beings' fundamental spiritual needs are: 1) **the need for an experience or belief in a supreme power that transcends the physical world;** 2) **the need for a sense of meaning, purpose, and value in one's existence,** and 3) **the need for a deep trust and relatedness to life,**

the experience of being part of the whole universe. Only when these three needs are met will we be complete and free.

Conclusion

Addiction is a desperate call to come home. When addictive thinking and behavior become the controlling force in our lives, we become powerless because of the nullification and replacement of our innermost self with a conditioned false-self. The false-self becomes our mask or persona—our identity of who we thought we were since childhood.

When addictions and dependencies control our lives and our life becomes unmanageable, it is a wake-up call for us to look in the mirror and see the mask that we are wearing and begin to realize that who we thought we were all our lives may not be a true representation of who we really are according to our spiritual blueprint that determines our potential purpose and destiny that we bring into the world. Addiction is a condition that separates us from our spiritual path to self-realization. This is why Twelve Step programs acknowledge addiction as a spiritual problem or spiritual bankruptcy that requires a spiritual solution in order to heal.

I think it is important to realize that it is not only people who are afflicted with chemical dependency that are in a state of spiritual crisis. In my opinion most, if not all, people born in our culture are affected by the cultural disease of *dis-ease*.

It is a systemic condition of our culture that manifests into an addictive thought-system that is the product of the addiction process. The addiction process is created from the beliefs and old ideas of the cultural psyche. Alcohol, drugs, and other addictions are aspects of the addiction process and thought-system that cause problems of living and death. The addiction process affects everyone in society on some level. The only factor that distinguishes chemically dependent persons from the rest of society is the biological or genetic component of the multi-dimensional disease model of addiction that we saw in

Fig. 1. But as we know from the disease model, the biological component is not the total picture. The primary component and problem of all addictions is the *psycho/spiritual* component of the disease model. This component is the result of the culturalization process and is responsible for the separation from our *innermost self*, from which we all suffer in our society.

The separation from our *innermost self*, or sacredness, causes us to seek a Higher Self, or God, in all forms of addictive behavior. Bill W., cofounder of Alcoholics Anonymous, once said that alcoholics are looking for God in the bottle. As addicts, we are looking for the lost self-the essence of our *being*. Unfortunately, our addiction is an inappropriate and self-destructive way to do this, and it continues to reinforce the separation. The emptiness that many of us felt during the years of addiction was the loss of *self*, but instead of staying with the feeling, we filled the emptiness with people, places, situations, and things, including alcohol, drugs, food, and other activities, which only gave us a false sense of self.

It is my opinion that because of our separation or loss of *self*, we as a culturalized society are in a spiritual crisis or emergency that needs spiritual CPR as soon as possible before we lose our humanity. This spiritual crisis or emergency usually results in what is called "hitting bottom," which is the same as the death of the inflated ego personality or false-self. For many people, this is the birth of a "Higher Self."

A personal spiritual emergency usually takes some kind of traumatic intervention in our life, such as a loss of a loved one, a threatening illness, or a personal crisis, such as going to jail, getting a divorce, or having an accident. Until this happens we will not experience our "bottom line" that serves as a wake-up call for us to surrender to the illusory sense of control and security that is created by our false-self from the attachment to past beliefs and old ideas.

Once we experience the birth of a Higher Self after hitting bottom, we need to immediately get into a spiritual program that will nurture and cultivate that Higher Self with spiritual principles that will guide us back home to our *innermost self* or divinity.

It is important to practice spiritual principles in our daily lives that will help us examine everything we have learned in our past and that will give us the insight to know that we must unlearn our past conditioned beliefs, ideas, and principles that have reinforced our separation from our soul. The practicing of spiritual principles in our daily lives will guide and help us to become aware of the benefits of living life on life's terms and experience the totality and divinity of life. This personal experience will expand our perception of reality by providing the fertile soil for a new way of thinking to emerge that will become the guiding light in finding our path to *self realization*.

When we begin to experience this process of *spiritual awakening*, the need to escape from the natural events of life by using mood-altering substances and activities will no longer be necessary. Then the only thing to drink to the point of intoxication is the joyfulness and beauty of life's divinity. Welcome home!

Appendices

Appendix I: Profile of Addiction

The risk of who will become an alcohol and other drug abuser/addict is influenced by childhood conditioning that is rigidly and narrowly formed and they are unable to adjust to the complex array of stresses in their world of perception. This is a very common form of emotional abuse and in many cases coupled with physical abuse that is prominent in child rearing with many families as a way of developing child obedience. Past studies have indicated that children who are more likely to become teenage drug abusers have low self-esteem, and are usually unsuccessful planners and decision makers who impress others with poor judgment. They usually resist rules and authority and instead are strongly seeking pleasure — often at any expense.

There are two powerful physical differences that make one young person more likely to turn to substance abuse and to keep on using and abusing them.

1—children who have higher rates for "addictive propensity" when their brain structure limits their capacities to feel rewarded due to high levels of stress hormones such as cortisol and/or abnormally low levels of dopamine function are high risk to turn to alcohol/drugs to self-medicate.
2—children who are highly anxious, repeatedly reporting feelings of sadness and hopelessness or are unable to stay with ideas or activities

long—example are children with Attention Deficit Hyperactivity disorder (ADHA)—are at hight risk for addiciton. These genetic and psychologically developed disorders limit how one chooses to find what activities and ideas can produce happiness and thus make these children more at risk for unhealthy motivations to find joy.

Addiction causes long-term, sometimes irreversible, changes in a teen's brain chemistry. This means many drugs change the way the brain functions, even when the person stops, or is prevented from, taking drugs. Drub abuse and addiciton are chronic conditions.

Many experts conclude the alcohol/drug addiction is primarily a complicated motivational handicap. An abuser or addict cannot detach from substance abuse if nothing else will produce pleasure.

Drug addictions frequently lose their strength and appeal when other interests and activites are discovered that replaces the alcohol/drug activity that are fulfilling and enjoyable conversion. This is sometimes called *"the bottom line"* when the abuser is *"sick and tired of being sick and tired."*

Many young people as well as adult abusers/addicts are able to create new and healthy balances between their judgement and pleasure centers in their brain by changing past thinking patterns. This happens in many cases in recovery programs that emphasize a spiritual dimension as the core issue of addiction.

Appendix II: Three-Step Exercise Ritual

This is a three-step exercise ritual that will assist you in letting go of your conditioned beliefs and old ideas that have kept you separated to the point of disconnection from your authentic or innermost self since childhood. This disconnection is that emptiness we have all felt most of our lives that we have filled with alcohol, drugs, food, sex, people, places, and things. It is the place where dis-ease lies and gnaws at our minds.

To begin the process of reconnection with your innermost self you will need some plain notebook paper or a journal for this spiritual journey. The first step is to list all your conscious beliefs. You may want to take a few days to do this because many of your beliefs are subtle and are just beneath the surface of awareness. After you have listed all the beliefs that you can remember, put your list away and don't think about it for a few days. After some time has passed, get out your list and review it and add any other beliefs that come to mind. Repeat this process every couple of days until you have listed all the beliefs you can remember. Next, examine your list and check off the beliefs that you feel have a limiting effect on your life or are no longer beneficial to you. Take a few minutes to contemplate on these beliefs. Now imagine living your life without them. Write down in your spiritual journal how it feels. Repeat this process every few days for the next two or three weeks, and then decide if you are convinced you want these beliefs out of your life. If your decision is to let go of these beliefs, you are now ready to go on to the second step.

On a separate piece of paper, write down the beliefs you have decided you no longer want in your life. Get a dish or some other inflammable container and a match. Place the container and belief list on a table in front of you. With your hands clasped together, as in prayer, bow your head and repeat the following affirmation of gratefulness: "You have served me well in my past, and I now release you from your service." Repeat this affirmation three times. Now light the paper, holding it over the dish, and repeat the following affirmation three times: "The burning of these beliefs is a process toward my spiritual awakening that will free me from the chains of bondage from my past conditioning."

Now you are ready for the third and final step—releasing the ashes to the wind. You can do this at some special place that gives you a feeling of spirituality or sacredness, or it can be your backyard. As you release the ashes to the wind, repeat three times: "I release these ashes of my past beliefs to their rightful place in the cosmos."

It is important to realize that your beliefs have been conditioned in your mind from a very young age. They have had years to sink deep into your psyche below the level of consciousness. You may want to repeat the ritual exercise as you become aware of more beliefs and old ideas that you no longer want in your life. As you repeat the exercise several times over a period of a few months, you may begin to feel relief from the weight of carrying all your past conditioned beliefs and feel a sense of liberation. As an on-going maintenance program to reinforce this freedom in your life, adopt the spiritual principles offered in the Twelve Steps and apply them in your daily life. I welcome you to the experience of change through the awakening process of recovery.

Appendix III: The Twelve Steps of AA

We—

1—Admitted we were powerless over alcohol—that our lives had become unmanageable.

2—Came to believe that a Power greater than ourselves could restore us to sanity.

3—Made a decision to turn our will and our lives over to the care of God as we understand Him.

4—Made a searching and fearless moral inventory of ourselves.

5—Admitted to God, to ourselves, and to another human being the exact nature of our wrongs.

6—Were entirely ready to have God remove all these defects of character.

7—Humbly asked Him to remove our shortcomings.

8—Made a list of all persons we had harmed and became willing to make amends to them all.

9—Made direct amends to such people wherever possible, except when to do so would injure them or others.

10—Continued to take personal inventory, and when we were wrong, promptly admitted it.

11—Sought through prayer and meditation to improve our conscious contact with God, *as we understood him*, praying only for knowledge of His will for us and the power to carry that out.

12—Having had a spiritual awakening as the result of these steps, we tried to carry this message to alcoholics and to practice these principles in all our daily affairs.

Appendix IV: The Twelve Steps of DA
(Dependencies Anonymous)

1—We admitted that we were powerless over our past conditioning, beliefs, and dependencies—that our life had become unmanageable.
2—We came to believe that a Power greater than ourselves could restore us to sanity.
3—We made a decision to turn our will and our life over to the care of God as we understand God.
4—We made a searching and fearless moral inventory of ourselves.
5—We admitted to God, to ourselves, and to another human being the exact nature of our wrongs.
6—We were entirely ready to have God remove all these defects of character.
7—We humbly asked God to remove our shortcomings.
8—We made a list of all persons we had harmed and became willing to make amends to them all.
9—We made direct amends to such people wherever possible, except when to do so would injure them or others.
10—We continued to take personal inventory, and when we were wrong, promptly admitted it.
11—We sought through prayer and meditation to improve our conscious contact with God, as we understood God, praying only for knowledge of God's will for us and the power to carry it out.
12—Having had a spiritual awakening as the result of these steps, we tried to carry this message to others and to practice these principles in all our affairs.

NOTE: These Twelve Steps have been adapted from the Twelve Steps of Alcoholics Anonymous.

Appendix V: Twelve Step Support Groups

Secular Groups

Adult Children of Alcoholics
Central Service Board
P.O. Box 3216
Torrance, California 90505
(310) 534-1815

Al-Anon/Alateen
Family Group Headquarters, Inc.
862 Midtown Station
New York, New York 10018
(212) 302-7240

Alcoholics Anonymous
World Services, Inc.
468 Park Avenue South
New York, New York 10016
(212) 686-1100

Co-Dependents Anonymous
P.O. Box 33577
Phoenix, Arizona 85067-3577
(602) 277-7991

Debtors Anonymous
P.O. Box 20322

New York, New York 10025-9992
(212) 642-8820

Gamblers Anonymous
P.O. Box 17173
Los Angeles, California 90017
(213) 386-8789

Narcotics Anonymous
P.O. Box 9999
Van Nuys, California 91406
(818) 780-3951

National Association for Children of Alcoholics
11426 Rockville Pike, Suite 100
Rockville, Maryland 20852
(301) 468-0985

Overeaters Anonymous World Service Office
2190—190th Street
Torrance, California 90504
(310) 618-8835

Sexaholics Anonymous
P.O. Box 300
Simi Valley, California 93062
(805) 581-3343

Appendix VI: SUGGESTED READING

Goodwin, D. (1988) *Is Alcoholism Hereditary*, Ballantine Books, NY

Miller, A. (1983) *For Your Own Good*, the Noonday Press, NY

Ash, M. (1993) *The Zen of Recovery*, Jeremy P. Tarcher/Putman Book, NY

Ellsworth, B. (1988) *Living In Love Wtih Yourself*, Breakthrough Publishing, Salt Lake City, UT

Napier, N. (1997) *Sacred Practices for Conscious Living*, W. W. Norton, NY

Klaas, J. (1982) *The 12 Steps to Happiness*, Ballantine Books, NY

Ferrini, P. (1994) *Love Without Conditions*, Heartways Press, South Deerfield, MA

May, G. (1988) *Addiction of Grace*, Harper, San Francisco

Kavanaugh, P. (1992) *Magnificent Addiction*, Aslan Publishing, Lower Lake, CA

Friel, J&L (1988) *Adult Children: the Secrets of Dysfunctional Families*, Health Communications, Deerfield, FL

The National Center on Addiction and Substance Abuse at Columbia University (1998) *Behind Bars: Substance Abuse and Amercia's Prison Population*

About the Author

Bob Colonna, PhD, DD, C.A.S is a nationally certified addiction specialist who has been counseling in the field of chemical dependency for sixteen years. He received his doctorate in Psychology Counseling in 1985. He was awarded a Doctor of Divinity and was ordained as an Inner Faith Minister in 1995.

He started his personal journey of recovery in 1980 as a student of various spiritual philosophies of the world and the Twelve-Step program.

He hosted a radio talk show, "Off the Hook with Dr. Bob," that aired in the San Francisco Bay Area and Northern California from 1991-93. He served as a hospice chaplain to the death and dying and was published in the 1992-93 edition of "Who's Who in the West" for his commitment to human services.

John Bradshaw, in a 1991 radio interview, was quoted as saying that "Dr. Bob is one of the innovative pioneers in the field of addiction who has the courage and insight to confront the real issues about addiction and will discuss them with anyone who is willing to listen."

Dr. Bob is available for lectures and workshops.

Book Order Information

To order one or more copies of the Web Published softcover bound book, contact: ***www.buybooksontheweb.com*** or ***Amazon.com***.

For information on the two-hour *Expect a Miracle* live lecture based on an expanded version of the book *The Addiction Process: A Systemic Cultural Condition* and/or audio cassette version, contact: **call** **1-510-595-5557**

For more copies, contact www.iUniverse.com.

For further information, contact:

> "Dr. Bob" Productions
> 1090 B St., #109
> Hayward CA 94541